INTRODUCTION

I dedicate this book to women everywhere who look in the mirror and say
"What the hell happened to me?"

What happened to the hot girl who turned guys' heads by cradling her perky breasts in body hugging halter-tops and her tight butt in sexy low-rise jeans?

Well, she writes a book and hopes that women will turn the pages and belly laugh to her memoirs of **Then and Now**.

I am not aspiring to be the next J.K Rowling or E.L. James.

I am just a middle-aged woman who needs to pay off some bills and student loans.

What's with that initial thing anyway?

I am Jane.

Plain Jane you say?

Hell no.

ACKNOWLEDGEMENTS

Hugs and kisses to my family and friends who believed in me and who pursued my writing dream with me. My goal is to make people laugh because when you laugh your worries and fears become lost in that moment of time. Humor is our natural defense against an ever changing world. If I filled your heart with laughter, then writing this book was my gift to you.

My father is my heavenly angel and it's through him that I received my sense of humor. My father's stories were so funny that people wanted and needed to hear them over and over again. Dad, I love you and miss you every day.

POCKETBOOK THEN

POCKETBOOK NOW

POCKETBOOK: THEN

A decorated denim purse, slung over my shoulder, housed a driver's license, eyeliner and a small white pleather wallet with a couple dollar bills, boyfriend's pictures, and some change. I left the money woes to the high school guys whose heads were still turned checking me out. Those boobies smothered with long, sun kissed hair could get me anything my heart, no, anything my rack desired. Bernie Madoff would be proud….money for nothing. The driver's license wasn't attached to any car it just served as a drinking ID for an 18 year old girl. Photo booth keepsakes were occasionally tossed in the purse if the night included a stroll on the boardwalk. These mini-strip pictures implied an unspoken permission for a French kiss or a quick body feel so facial side views were the norm.

POCKETBOOK: NOW

I now harness a sack that could transport two Great Danes. Screw Hollywood celebrities and their miniscule pooch purses. The 50 something pocketbook includes body lotion, feminine napkins for a possible leak (nothing to do with a monthly cycle), safety pins, Band-Aids, wristlet and credit card purse (these purses can be utilized when the sack is left in the car), hairbrush, make-up bag, keys and spare keys, tissues, receipts, drink tokens from various drinking establishments, chewing gum, mints, matches, hand sanitizer, iPhone charger, eye drops, an impressive selection of pharmaceuticals, coupons, calendar/daily planner, checkbook, sunglasses/glasses, pens, contact lens case, and a mirror.

I realize the military gear, strapped across my chest, is jockeying for position with an angry push-up bra. The only head turning from the boys now is when they mumble, "WTF lady," after the sack bumps against their tanned and toned muscular bodies. Damn, these impure thoughts are nothing but a free pass to Purgatory. Wait, is there a Purgatory anymore?

I guess this sack is symbolic of the three baby boys that destroyed my once healthy uterus. At least that's what I expect my therapist to say when I'm straddling a brown leather chair.

BODY HEAT THEN

BODY HEAT NOW

BODY HEAT: THEN

My teen years recognized that sweating was bothersome but taking a cool shower, jumping in a pool, or swimming in the ocean remedied the situation. I will admit that waitressing in a pancake house, without air conditioning, was horrible but sweating in my polyester white uniform gave me power. We didn't need a Hooters logo because we had the heat. Families waited in long lines for tables and until this very moment, I thought our breakfast menu kicked ass. It was the servers' sweaty uniforms that showed some ass. The heat presented me with "daddy porn" tips. Those tips supported my higher education degree.

BODY HEAT: NOW

I am living in a 24/7 volcanic eruption. Heat has taken on a whole new territory. It's called men-o-pause. That's right everything appalling in a woman's life begins with the word men. Men-stru-ation, men-tal illness, men-orrhea. Go ahead, Google the word menorrhea. You know you want to.

I sleep in pajama shorts and a tank top year round. I wear the classic winter apparel to bed but when the tropical rainforest tiptoes into my bedroom, I slither from my bed sensing a tsunami has thrown up on me. My fingers poke at matted hair, soaking wet clothes, swamp ass and a flushed face that could light any chiminea. The sweating is alarmingly intense and I grab for the spare shorts and tank top cradled in the sliding caddy under my personal tomb. I crawl back into bed as an overpowering chill embraces my entire being.

My bedroom is now Antarctica because menopause is fucking with me. I scurry beneath the sheets and blankets to thaw my freezing body. The thawing lasts for approximately 5 minutes when again men-o-pause screws with me. The blankets and sheets are tossed in the air like a frustrated pizza maker.

Daytime menopause means never wearing anything that frames the neck. Shirts and blouses are identified as prostitute professional because the breast exposure could be viewed as taxable income by those unfamiliar with a woman's change of life. A personal fan hovers by so the fiery face can ingest the whirling blades of wind. God forgive the person who unintentionally stands in front of the life-saving appliance.

A hot flash is life's way of punishing women for ever complaining about menstrual cramps. Nature is saying, "What's up girl? You moan when you **have** a period and groan when you **don't have** a period." Do not let your man read that last line or you'll be hearing it as he breathes his last breath. In fact, he should be worshipping menopause because it prevents his beloved balls from going under the knife. By the way, has anyone seen my fucking fan? I regret my sometimes-tasteless language but when a hot flash hits, there's no apologizing.

MAKE-UP THEN

MAKE-UP NOW

MAKEUP: THEN

A black eyeliner pencil and a tube of black mascara rocked a velvety smooth face. These particulars, along with a wild messy mane, made a girl feel like a sexy Farrah Fawcett pin-up poster. Teen lips have a natural pink sheen of their own so lipstick and gloss weren't adolescent beauty essentials. My makeup application was short and simple.

MAKEUP: NOW

A lighted miner's helmet is required to locate concealer, primer, moisturizer, eyeliner, eye shadow, foundation, blush, mascara, an eyelash curler, lip liner, lipstick, lip gloss, and lip filler that bottom feed in the bottom of my cosmetics bag. Unfortunately, the lip filler is useless. Can somebody please tell me how these incisions encircling my mouth got there? Exactly who is responsible for these separations of skin? The tooth fairy leaves money for teeth but this nighttime son-of-a-bitch takes my youth and leaves permanent slits. Excuse my language, just the menopause talking.

My morning routine includes painting my face. I perform this face painting ritual because I don't want people repulsed by having to look at my colorless skin. After all, your face does make the first impression and it's important to look good because like it or not, a man gazes at you with his eyes, not with his brain or the other below the Mason-Dixon Line thing. It's funny; I just realized that I wore makeup as a teen-ager so I could look older now I'm a middle-aged woman wearing makeup so I can look younger.

The parade of cosmetics begins with a mixing of vitamin B brightening cream and a hydrating foundation primer. The progression continues with a liquid foundation that promises to lift my face as it smooths and firms.

I once dreamt that I was trapped on a connect the dots coloring book page and my facial skin was being lifted as I penciled in lines from number to number. Damn, I have to search dream interpretation sites and have my mind's hidden message analyzed. I can imagine the breakdown now, "You have lines, wrinkles, and deep creases permanently engraved on your age appropriate face. As far as *connecting the dots*, your dreams connect to reality and the reality is that the only person looking closely at your 50 something face is your dermatologist. Therefore, stay *connected* to him."

I started using eye shadow after glancing in the mirror and noticing that my eyelids were sitting on my eyelashes. I wanted my eyelids to be more noticeable so I settled on a trio of light to medium brown powders. I experimented with the sparkly, much brighter cream shadows but they made me look like a schizophrenic clown who couldn't decide if she belonged in the circus or hustling on the streets.

Next, black eyeliner. An endearing quality of eyeliner is how it adds depth to my lashes making them appear thicker and sexier. I tried sporting the youthful, smoky look one day but a student asked me why my eyes were black and blue. The *punched in the eye* critique wasn't exactly what I was expecting. I stick to the straight-line application because it doesn't take much time or effort and it always looks fashionable. Why reinvent the wheel?

If stranded on a desert island with only one make-up product, it would have to be my waterproof black mascara. Mascara gives me mile long lashes with just the flip of a wand. Waterproof is a must because my fluctuating hormones produce spontaneous crying sessions that could leave me looking like Tammy Faye Bakker if not for the impermeable mascara.

Lip liner and lipstick are added to my colorful canvas. I outline my lips with a neutral color because of a comment made by a guy years ago. It grossed him out looking at an older woman's mouth because her lipstick bled into the lines and crevasses surrounding her lips. I am that older woman now and I'll be damned if my lips are going to bleed.

I employ a lip color that promises 16 hours of comfortable wear. No touch-ups are required even after meals. I must admit, I have been using this lip color for many years and it does stay on all day. Oh, by the way, this product is definitely a kiss proof lip color. You can tongue plunge all you want while never leaving your color on him. Wait; let me read that last sentence again. Wow, that's a great advertising slogan for my 16-hour lip color. Am I right or what?

Finally, blush's purpose is to add soft color and highlights to the cheek area. There are too many women managing blush like a Crayola crayon, coloring in their entire face. They get that, "Hey look at me, I've developed rosacea thing going on."

FACIAL HAIR THEN

FACIAL HAIR NOW

I hate it when
you offer someone
a sincere compliment
on their moustache
and suddenly . . .

She's not your
friend anymore.

FACIAL HAIR: THEN

I didn't even know women had facial hair. I had the Brooke Shields "no need to pluck your eyebrows" look complemented by a peachy cream complexion or a golden summer tan. The only facial hair I knew was the five o'clock shadow that adorned John Travolta's strikingly handsome face. That was hot. I realize many of you are thinking, "What about beard burn?" I hear you, girl; I'm just not listening. Any facial rash gifted by a Vinnie Barbarino look alike was comparable to winning a Willy Wonka golden ticket.

FACIAL HAIR: NOW

My face harbors a peach plantation in which one black hair strategically nestles on the bottom of my chin. A construction worker's pliers are required to remove the vexing hair. If fingers tug at the single whisker, it will curl and predictably become a ghastly pubic hair. My fifty something years thank the Vietnamese girls, at the nail salon, for taking waxing responsibilities for my upper lip and eyebrows. Do you think Brooke needs to pluck her bushy abnormally thick eyebrows yet? Sorry, Brooke. It's the menopause talking. Did I mention menopause before? I seriously can't remember.

HAIR THEN

HAIR NOW

HAIR: THEN

I had long brown hair with a twinkle of gold dancing on each strand. In college, I started highlighting my locks because the effects of the summer sun grew out making my mane appear two- toned. Hair products included whatever shampoo my mother had in the shower. I washed my hair scrunched it between my fingers and for the special occasions blew it out and activated my hot rollers. My guy friends loved running their carnal fingers through it. I guess it was a cheap aphrodisiac for a male teen. It got things going….you know what I mean.

HAIR NOW:

I hate my hair! Those long luscious tresses are now baby fine threads that form a bird's nest in the nape of my neck. I guess it's the result of years of abuse with highlights, perms, curling irons, hair straighteners, and blow dryers. I had a perm one time that was concocted in a friend's basement salon. She had her cosmetology license but I guess the wine we consumed was more important than paying attention to some insignificant hair timer. My scalp was charred but the alcohol made me confident as I sashayed down the street flipping my sheep's fleece from side to side. If a guy slipped his hand through my pristine perm, lubricating oil would be needed to free his toxic fingers.

I've tried so many hair products, from friends' recommendations, but most of the stuff ends up in my trashcan. Hair sprays piss me off almost as much as menopause. We have freeze spray, extreme spray, ultra hold spray, super hold spray, extra firm spray, leave in spray, curl shaping spray, flat iron spray and weightless spray to name a few. Now, if I really believed that weightless spray claim, I'd spray that witch's brew all over my sagging, aging body. Fuuuuck, a hot flash is coming on because my wayward vocabulary is rearing its ugly head.

BATHING SUIT THEN

BATHING SUIT NOW

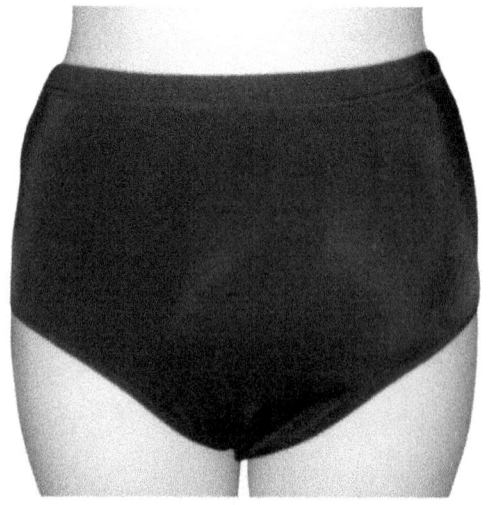

BATHING SUIT: THEN

Buying a bathing suit in my teens was simple. I'd go to the store, pick out a bikini, try it on, and run to the register. Solid colors always looked sexy on a sun kissed body. I even shimmied down the runway sporting a white bikini in a local beauty pageant. I didn't take the crown and it's my professional opinion that the judges were former weight watcher clients and jealous little bitches. That's my story and I'm sticking to it. Oh, that thing about diamonds being a girl's best friend is a lie. We all know that a bikini is a girl's best friend and it's the bikini that motivates a guy's penis to tell his brain to purchase those expensive timeless jewels.

BATHING SUIT: NOW

Purchasing a bathing suit is a 9 to 5 job. Ill-fated hours are devoted to dressing room mirrors and hidden tears. My living hell is seeing my reflection in a four way mirror. Not only is the muffin top exposed but also the sagging behind, droopy boobs and fatty back rolls. Xanax is essential when bathing suit shopping. It takes the edge off as well as a few delusional pounds. I normally sport a black on black tankini. Fifty something girls know that wearing black deducts at least 20 pounds from the troubled tummy area. Middle finger accolades to the genius who coined the word tankini because shrouding our bodies in a tankini is simply stuffing menopausal baby fat into a wife beater spandex tee and granny panties (bikini bottoms my ass). And, why isn't the tankini just called a **big**ini? I guess that would be politically incorrect.

JEANS THEN

JEANS NOW

JEANS: THEN

Low rise, hip hugging, bell-bottom jeans coddled my young teen body and the guys went nuts whenever I wore a halter-top or tube top with them. The boys didn't appreciate it when the 70's girls wore body suits with their hip huggers because body suits, with their snaps and crotch hooks, were birth control friendly. The cool thing about wearing the body suit, with the low rise jeans, was that you never had to worry about being over-exposed. Everything was tucked neatly away. You did have to worry about having an attractive figure though because body suits showed every line, roll and crease. Not a problem for me back then.

My boyfriend would *pitch a tent* every time I bent over in my hipster jeans. I knew how to bend and snap long before Reese Witherspoon (Legally Blonde) ever took a lesson. Too bad, I didn't stockpile those high school jeans because the low rise has made a comeback with a more expensive price tag.

JEANS: NOW

Where do I begin? There are so many styles of jeans to wear as a mature woman. Not Your Daughter's jeans, I Don't have a Daughter's jeans and WTF are Daughter's jeans? I love the labels that promise you'll look 10 pounds thinner in ten seconds jeans. There is so much hidden elastic in the middle-aged woman's jeans that if yanked high enough they could double as a push-up bra. Take notice that I am cautioning any girls who wore the low rise, bell bottom jeans then, not to wear them now. Adult women need to realize that our middle and backside areas do not allow for below the belly button jeans. These areas require complete coverage because they are zoned eye cabbage, not eye candy. Nobody needs to see butt crack or a sex area that looks like an ad for Miracle-Gro. And as far as wearing a body suit today, I could wear one on Halloween and go out as a Japanese sumo wrestler.

Spandex, the God of synthetic fibers, known for its exceptional flexibility, is found in skinny jeans. I have to admit that my gams look great in skinny jeans as long as my muffin top is camouflaged under some loose fitting shirt. People compliment me on my *Tina Turner* legs but my oldest son remarked that my legs are so muscular, that I could play the fullback position on any NFL team. And to think that I provided him a womb for nine months and had to suffer in pain for 18 hours before receiving saddle block anesthesia that could have caused nerve damage leading to long-lasting numbness and pain or even worse, a seizure or heart attack. There's nothing better than laying a guilt trip on your child, but with my boys, it never works. Their usual response is, "Well, that's your job", and "Stop, you're so gross", or "You're the reason I'll being seeing a psychiatrist one day."

So, as far as spandex, a middle-aged woman needs to use caution when purchasing jeans. A little spandex goes a long way. I put my spandex jeans on each morning and look fabulous but by mid-day, I'm picking them up from around my fucking ankles. I am not having a hot flash; it just ticks me off that some spandex jeans that cost a week's wages, especially ripped jeans, can leave me looking like a poser gangsta especially when the knot in my bandana slips around to the front of my head. Isn't it ironic that we purchase jeans with rips yet we throw out jeans that get holes in them? Damn, the price we pay to be fashionable. At least I'm not wearing the up to my chest elastic waist polyester pants with a tissue sticking out of the pockets...well...not yet anyway.

PHOTOGRAPHS THEN

PHOTOGRAPHS NOW

PHOTOGRAPHS: THEN

Thanks to the Kodak film industry for providing photographs of personal, celebratory times in life. The times known as a *Kodak moment*. The moments captured on a roll of 24 exposures 35mm film. The film, if exposed to light, would be destroyed with all its precious memories. I remember panicking after opening the camera and discovering that the film was not completely wound into the canister. I shamelessly recalled blaming my friend for not rewinding the hand crank properly and discovered my vernacular contained words vomited by Linda Blair as her head rotated 360 degrees. Linda and I shared private exorcisms. She endured the devil and I bore blank film. On a positive note, taking pictures was normally quick with very little posing or positioning. My body was rock hard so it didn't matter *how I stood* or *where I stood* for a photo.

PHOTOGRAPHS: NOW

Where do I begin? Photographs today can be taken without my knowledge or permission. A split second snap turns into a permanent image on the internet or community cell phones. "What happens in Vegas stays in Vegas" attitude of earlier days is gone. I have to be watchful of everything I do when I'm out partying with the girls. For reasons unknown to me, I find my body slithering down chairs, tables, beams, and posts. My floorshow procures many barstool ovations but even I know the applause is due to the *no cover charge* entertainment. After all, it's the Happy Hour bunch.

One particular bar, that's close to my apartment, plays great dance music but attracts an over 60 crowd. I liked to walk to the inn and not worry about drinking and driving. Not to be conceited, but I am like Anne Margaret in the *Dirty Old Men* movie. When I start dancing, the men's phone cameras come out prompting the wives' and girlfriends to snag them away. The men are given a quiet lashing and heaven forbid if one of them approaches me to dance. I actually had a woman scold me for coming to the bar. She said that I didn't belong there and she didn't appreciate me dancing near her husband. I was only seven years younger than she was. The woman's a bitter old bitch who wears cracked ruby red lipstick and perfume that smells like a mothball attic.

When sober photographs are taken, I immediately go into the fashion model mode. I turn to the right and put my left leg to the front. I know from experience that my image appears thinner and more refined. My biggest setback is positioning my body before middle-aged female family and friends try to manipulate the desired zone. It's not unusual to take a woman's elbow to my chest or back while struggling for the perfect position. Don't mess with me when I am taking a picture for posterity or for Facebook. Damn, it's getting hot in here! Where is that delete button? I hate this fucking photo.

TELEPHONE THEN

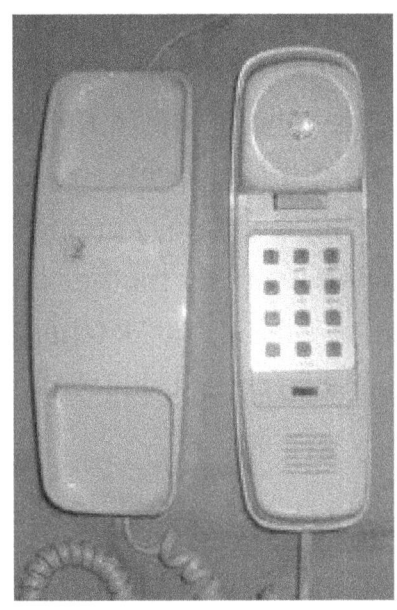

TELEPHONE NOW

TELEPHONE: THEN

I could care less about the telephone during my teenage years. I was always with my friends so there was no need to call them. We discussed, at night, what we would do the following day. The telephone was used if plans had to be changed. The pay phone, down the street, was utilized when I didn't want my parents to know what I was planning or scheming. The family phone was cradled in its' base, on the kitchen wall. My mother and her bunny ears overheard anything said in that kitchen. I'll tell you, that woman could hear a lie being told from hell.

TELEPHONE: NOW

I love that I can communicate with my thumbs. Wait, who the hell am I kidding? I peck at that cruel keyboard with my right index finger while my eyes are glued to spellcheck. I am tired of being embarrassed by words and phrases that were not my intentions. I once text that I was having a drink on a deck but in spellcheck world, I had a drink on a dick. Excuses for spellcheck are mute when people sense a sexual overtone. They continue to reply with suggestive texts until someone senses imminent danger on the job or in the home. The delete icon is pushed more frequently than shoppers on Black Friday.

The iPhone is my only means of communication. If my smartphone is out of reach, I shake like a prostitute who's cheated her pimp. Before the smartphone, I would spend hours talking on my phone. Now, if someone calls me, I reply with a text. And, for numbers that I don't recognize, they have a better chance of being adopted by Brad Pitt and Angeline Jolie than of me answering the phone. My motto is, "If it's that important they can leave a message."

A few months back, I misplaced my iPhone at school. At the time, I didn't have a password lock and my life was out there for all to see. My panic was nothing short of a heart attack imagining some student hysterically laughing at my *glamour* shots and reading my delicate texts and emails. Once discovered, my private photos and words would pop up on every cell phone in school. Cameron Diaz had nothing on this *Bad Teacher*. Her cinematic character, once fictional, was now reality and I was playing the lead role. There was nothing immoral or criminal on my phone just some embarrassing and awkward particulars that only I should see.

I ran to the Media Center because I was using my iPhone to help my students locate information for their PowerPoint presentations. I checked the area between each computer and surveyed every table and chair. I inquired at the front desk but the elderly woman said that the students had not turned in an iPhone. No duh, like a teenager is ever turning in a staff member's phone.

I sauntered back to my classroom feeling like Eeyore the pessimistic, gloomy old donkey from Winnie the Pooh. Eeyore was depressed because his tail was attached to his backside with a pushpin and I was depressed because I was about to become the laughing stock of the school and community. Poor me, what to do. Class was about to begin when I noticed a blue bag with a peace sign on it. I tore through that bag like a sugar-crazed child on Halloween. There it was, resting in the bottom of my bag, my iPhone. Menopause was *effing* with me once again. I had completely forgotten that I had taken the blue bag to the Media Center to could collect my students' hard copies and notes. I like the word *effing* because it's more lady like than saying fucking. A family member's unfavorable review of my cursing is stuck in my head.

MULTITASKING THEN

MULTITASKING NOW

MULTITASKING: THEN

I didn't need to stick post-its on my dashboard and forehead or wrap a string around my finger because I clearly remembered everything I needed to do. Multitasking was easy for me but my young brain performed more efficiently and more effectively when I concentrated on one task at a time. That was my choice. My mind was in perfect harmony with my body and soul. Homework, athletics, boyfriends, friends, work, and social events all held their order of importance in my daily schedule. Unlike teens who could study while blasting hard rock music, I required quiet surroundings to achieve academic success. I owe my steadfast study habits to the Sisters of Saint Joseph.

I attended a Catholic elementary school and two years of Catholic high school, before my family moved to New Jersey. I can tell you those nuns had 40-50 students in class yet everyone learned to read, write, and perform mathematical computations. Testing standards were never lowered and *study buddies* weren't necessary. The sisters prided themselves on classroom control but control was a given since the boys and girls sat eye to eye with Jesus hanging on a large crucifix believing the nun's claim that the eyes in the back of her head were hidden under her long black veil.

The nuns demanded and expected academic excellence, with no nonsense behavior, and they got it. Nuns didn't have to deal with Boards of Education or school administrators. If parents had a problem with corporal punishment, they could request their student's transcripts and register the expendable child with the neighborhood public school. In all honesty, those nuns provided me with the educational tools necessary to succeed academically.

I am laughing out loud because menopause has destroyed me. My mind drifted from multitasking to elementary school. Oh well, the paragraphs stay because it's living proof of how my golden years are greedily consuming my thoughts and words. I'm an effing mess. Notice I didn't use the "F" word because nuns are the religious Santa Claus. They know when you are sleeping, they know when you're awake, they know if you've been bad or good so be good for goodness sake. Amen to that.

MULTITASKING: NOW

X-rays of my brain today would reveal a rat maze similar to those used in biological research labs. The difference being, there is no victory cheese waiting at the end of my twisting path, just a box filled with jumbled thoughts, floating in a half century old head. I find myself mentally exhausted after completing a simple task only to find that I had been working on 10 other things at the same time. I was so disgusted with myself one day that I backtracked and wrote down the goings-on within my menopausal mind.

It was a beautiful, wintry Saturday morning and I opened my laptop to check my AOL mail. I know I am showing my age with AOL mail. I can't help it. I started using AOL many years ago and I refuse to switch now. At least dial-up is gone and I don't have to watch that little yellow guy running across the screen accompanied by nail biting screeching and hissing sounds. Come on, be honest, you probably have that melody rooted in your brain and could repeat it verbatim. I'll be damned. There I go again. My mind drifted from the 10 activities that I was listing to initiating a history lesson about AOL. Let me try this once more.

I opened my email to find a letter from my friend asking if we could get together for her birthday. I had all intentions of answering her, but instead, ran for a pen to mark the date on my large wall calendar. I couldn't find a working pen so I decided to make myself a cup of tea. I poured the water into my cup but my son called, so, I answered the phone. My sister was beeping in while I was talking to him, so, I put him on hold. I spoke to my sister, forgot about my son, and hung up on her because the UPS carrier was knocking at my door. He handed me a box, which I started to open when my sister phoned back and asked why I had hung up on her. The box was half-open but I dismissed it because my sister was giving me a crockpot recipe and I had to add the ingredients to my shopping list. I picked up the pen to find it would not write and remembered that I attempted to use it an hour ago when I hoped to write my friend's birthday on my calendar. I feel exhausted after reading what I have written and my tea is now ice cold. I wouldn't recall having hot tea if the untouched cup wasn't staring me in the face.

SEX THEN

SEX NOW

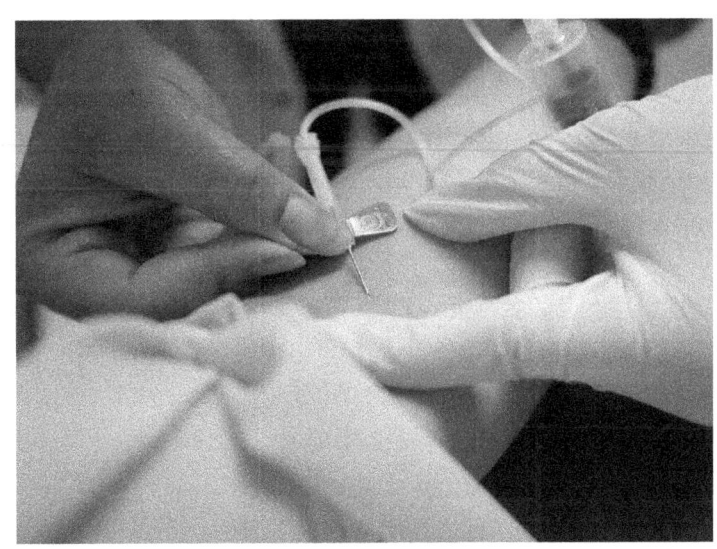

SEX: THEN

Regrettably, I had only one lover who became my husband and eventually my ex-husband. Monogamy didn't provide for much promiscuity accompanied by the fact that we both attended the same high school and college. We performed the basic foreplay and missionary positions with the occasional role-play being performed on a drinking night. My favorite personalities were the cowboy and cowgirl, the explorer and the native and the teacher and student. High school and college went by so fast and it's as if my boyfriend and I were game pieces on a Monopoly board and our lives were being played out in some systematic way.

My college roommates were disgusted that I was a one-man woman so they occasionally, under the influence, invited men to sleep with me. Their plan never reached fruition so they finally gave up on their feeble attempts to liberate me from my vow of chastity. My friends were under the impression that having one sex partner was equivalent to a life of virginity since I had nothing else to compare *it* to.

My eldest sister, she's 14 months older than me, was my teen idol. She dressed fashionably and played an awesome guitar. She performed the coolest rendition of *House of the Rising Sun*. I achieved academic A's but she scored impressive grades outside the classroom door.

My sister worked at a store that sold numerous varieties of chocolates, candies, nuts, and peanuts. She managed to work, do homework, and take violin lessons without a single complaint. I asked if she could get me a job working with her and she did. My first retail career lasted a dismal three weeks.

On my fifth day at work, a soiled looking man stumbled to the counter and asked how much my nuts cost. I politely asked him which brand of nuts he was interested in buying. His response was loud and crude, "I want your nuts baby." I felt a surge of heat bouncing from my face as my eyes darted around the candy canisters searching for my sister. She was assisting another customer but the store manager saw my demise and ran to my rescue. The pervert hurried out the door with the manager on his tail. After the chase, my sister came over to where I was hiding and crying. She assured me that the man was just a harmless, local drunk and to be mindful that these things happen when you work in a city. I vowed that would never happen to me again, so, I put in my two-week notice.

Forgive me, but if that pervert spoke those words to me today, he'd be wearing his nuts around his neck, like a choker collar (size permitting). I guess you can say that I had my first sexual encounter at the "counter."

SEX: NOW

Sex in my fifties is life threatening. It's too risky and I don't want to die for a few minutes of pleasure. This is the crisis facing a divorced woman after 29 years of marriage. Grasping a fifty something penis is comparable to handling a grenade with a missing pin. Having sex with middle aged men is bedding every man and woman on earth. Nobody knows who or what these baby boomers have penetrated with their bruised bananas and dehydrated grapes. Any declaration of cleanliness is far from the truth and the only road to certainty is withholding sex until a blood test is administered. Damn, that 26 years of teaching is coming back to haunt me. I feel like I'm lecturing to my high school students. I even went so far as to joke with my family doctor about giving my name to single men who have a clean bill of health. He laughed but I know he must have been thinking, *just what I want to do, pimp out my female patients. Jane's a hot mess these days.*

 My younger sister delicately informed me that there are promiscuous cougars on the loose and requiring a blood test is a guarantee that I will spend the rest of my life alone. That statement seriously deflated my enthusiasm for intimacy. I really don't care because a high percentage of men, in their fifties, are on prescription drugs caused by high blood pressure, high cholesterol, depression, diabetes, anxiety, hormonal imbalances, and numerous psychological hang-ups. A low sex drive and dependency on Viagra are the results of these medical conditions. I'm sorry but after revisiting these past few sentences, I say,

"Screw it (no pun intended); I'd rather have a night stand filled with toys.

I tried online dating with hopes of finding true love. One guy profiled himself as a baseball pitcher and he looked HOT. I showed his photo to a friend and she laughed while telling me that this man used the same picture when she was on the site five years ago. I decided that she must have been mistaken so I accepted a date with him.

I made my sister and friend tag along. The girls dropped me off at the restaurant/bar and then drove to another pub down the road. They wanted me to have a great time and not worry about drinking and driving. I was instructed to text them when I was ready to go home.

The establishment was packed and my eyes scanned the room looking for my young Jim Palmer. I heard someone holler, "Yo, Jane." My handsome baseball player wore a comb over and sported a champion wattle. You know that hanging skin under a turkey's neck.

He introduced himself and informed me that he keeps an open bar tab for his dates but limits himself to two beers. He suggested a shot and a drink for me. A red flag shimmied up my erogenous pole and after one glass of wine, I text the girls to come and get me.

He reprimanded me when they came to the bar and maintained that bringing them along was childish. If it weren't for them, I might have been with child after possibly being roofied by the serial dater. He scared the sex out of me.

BLADDER AND GIRL STUFF THEN

BLADDER AND GIRL STUFF NOW

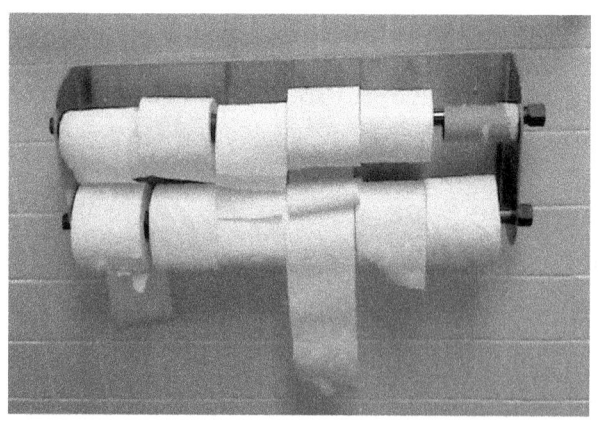

BLADDER AND GIRL STUFF: THEN

I didn't know or want to know about bladder issues when I was a teen-ager. I knew urinating was a bodily function but never gave it much thought. I do know that if I had to pee badly enough, squatting beside a car or a tree or relieving myself in a men's

room wasn't beneath me. The latter usually happened during a standing room only rock concert. I just went into the stall and had a guy friend guard the door for me. I guess urinating became an issue when I had my menstrual period (otherwise known as *your friend* in my house). Even then it wasn't a major concern because the XL tampons of long ago could hold back the Hoover Dam. I know those bad boys tore my hymen years before I became sexually active. The hymen is the petite piece of skin surrounding the vagina and if *broken* would be felt by your husband on your honeymoon night. That's right; the clueless groom would learn that he had just married the town tramp because that tiny opening had been compromised. Little did he know that the tampons his young bride had been vaginally inserting, for years, could split adjoined twins. By the way, did you know that a woman has two holes housed in her feminine parts? I did not.

BLADDER AND GIRL STUFF: NOW

OK, back to the holes concealed in a woman's feminine area. I am ashamed and embarrassed to say that I was 50 years old when I found out that girls have two holes down there. The conversation came up during lunch when I was discussing a medical procedure that I was undergoing for bladder concerns. There were five female friends at my table. I explained that a tube would be inserted into my vagina but I had no real worries because three babies had passed through that very same space. Well, the 20 something teacher practically fell off her chair laughing while tears rolled down her face and pieces of food slid through her teeth. She began to inform me and the other naive veteran teachers that urine comes from a totally different opening than does our monthly flow. The conversation turned comical with laughter so loud that it could be heard throughout the junior high school building. That night, in the privacy of my bathroom, I placed a hand held mirror down there to check for this second mysterious hole. Lo and behold, it was there. I shared the story with my urologist and he snickered while mentioning that one day he would like to have lunch with my friends and me.

My 50 something bladder is cruel. It controls my life. I sometimes have to avoid enjoyable social situations because of port-a-potties standing in for conventional bathrooms. The discomfort and urgent feeling "to go" is so intense that I find myself mapping out the nearest restrooms when I know I will be gathering with a large group of people. Every time I pass a public bathroom, I robotically go in and pee because there is never any question about me having to go. If I am traveling for more than an hour, the mode of transportation must include a bathroom or I will not go. Proof being, after drinking a large mug of tea, I boarded a bus to New York City. It was a two and a half hour journey and my bladder muscles gave way half way through the trip. I twisted my legs like a Pilate's instructor and approached the driver with tears in my eyes. There was no chance of him stopping at a rest area because the commuters were on a tight schedule and he was under the impression that they would drag him through the streets if they were late for work. When we finally reached our destination, I practically knocked over the other passengers as I bullied my way down the aisle from the back of the bus. And yes, I had droplets of pee in my panties before locating a ladies room. My first order of business was buying a new pair of underwear in the city.

One entry on my "bucket list" is to ring in the New Year in Times Square. I watch the New York City crowds cheering in the streets every December 31st and dream of the day that I will be standing there covered in confetti, kissing the love of my life. Then, my dream becomes a nightmare. I begin panicking about the nearest restrooms. I see the crowds immovable, elbow to elbow, without an inch of personal space between them. I imagine myself standing bowlegged in a urine soaked granny diaper with a chaffed wee-wee while intoxicated partiers scream, "What the hell is that smell?"

I am having a menopausal moment right now as I pull out my shirt and blow down on my chest. My face and neck are Rudolph red and water droplets are rolling down my face. And if that isn't enough, I have to pee. Son-of-a-bitch!

COLON THEN

COLON NOW

COLON: THEN

My colon was in total sync with my teenage body. I released my tootsie roll every morning and continued with my daily routine. Tootsie roll, how immature is that? I am smiling right now as I recall the ridiculous names that we give our solid waste. Names like: shit, poop, caca, dooky, turd, shitcicle, fudge, log, crap, loaf, boulder, dung, doo-doo, number two and Hershey bar to name a few. I can bet that you're probing your brain right now thinking about names you could add to the list. Go ahead; join in the fun because it will make you smile too. Probably the most famous fecal matter was, *Mr. Hankey, The Christmas Poo*. If you're not familiar with Mr. Hankey, I recommend you go to YouTube and search the *Mr. Hankey* song. There goes that teacher in me again. Once a teacher, always a teacher.

COLON: NOW

My colon is my internal enemy. I know it hates me. My only defense against this demon is the dreaded anti-diarrhea caplets. I have nightmares of standing in line, with a box of these *anal leakage blockers* while the cashier is screaming, to her colleague five aisles away, "How much for the 120 count diarrhea pills?"

I have consumed apples, fiber supplements, brown rice, bran cereal, whole grains, oatmeal, nuts, beans, and many other foods/supplements suggested on my online search of, "How to stop occasional diarrhea." Girlfriend, there is no stopping it. I've had colonoscopies but the findings are always this: I'm clean as a whistle. What the hell does that expression mean anyway? A whistle isn't clean. It's pressed between two lips while air is blown from the mouth into a tiny hollow cavity. I'm sorry but if my butt is as clean as a whistle, then I need to invest in a bidet, one of those tiny toilets that sprays water into an underwear's hidden area.

Wait, let's get back to colonoscopy; when do young men and women decide they want to become gastroenterologists and make a living sticking tubes up people's asses? And what exactly would the course of study be? **Finger Probing 101**, **Entering Through the Backdoor**, **Intro to Rectal Tubing and Plumbing**, **Polyps and Anal Prizes, Bowels and Aging Balls** and **Exploring the Hershey Highway**?

I know that spicy foods are my internal nemesis but I can't stop eating them. I am addicted and will accept the agonizing consequences in the bathroom afterwards. I eat hot chili, jalapenos, hot mustard, tabasco sauce, wasabi peanuts, hot wings, and spicy crab seasoning just to name a few. I even keep a shaker full of crushed red pepper on the kitchen table. Speaking of crabs, I recently had the pleasure of devouring two dozen blue claw crabs with my sister and her husband in a quaint shipping town café. The crabs were delicious but generously smothered with a fiery seafood spice.

My "boiler" started acting up immediately after the crab feast, resulting in belly bloating and intense abdominal discomfort. I hadn't eaten a spicy crab in over a year and I defied my inner conscience and plowed right in, mallet and all. I felt uncomfortable but it didn't stop me from completing a short pub-crawl.

This Irish pub had an awesome one-man band and his music was most definitely meant for dancing. Whenever I sensed an apparent gas attack, I boogied away from my friends, into a large group of people, so the smelly culprit could be one of many. It was anyone's guess but it certainly wasn't the sweet blonde smiling and moving sensually around the dance floor. I pride myself on how I can camouflage anything.

I went back to the hotel and fell asleep. At 3:30 in the morning, I awoke from my slumber to find myself bent over, at the waist, moaning like a dog in heat. I rushed to the vacant toilet with no time to spare. The remainder of the night was spent running in and out of the bathroom until my insides emptied out. I suppose spicy foods are Jane's kryptonite.

GROCERY SHOPPING THEN

GROCERY SHOPPING NOW

Nutrition Facts
Serving Size 1 cup 165g (165 g)

Amount Per Serving	
Calories 193	Calories from Fat 7
	% Daily Value*
Total Fat 1g	1%
Saturated Fat 0g	0%
Trans Fat	
Cholesterol 0mg	0%
Sodium 7mg	0%
Total Carbohydrate 44g	15%
Dietary Fiber 1g	4%
Sugars 0g	
Protein 4g	

Vitamin A	0%	Vitamin C	0%
Calcium	1%	Iron	16%

*Percent Daily Values are based on a 2,000 calorie diet. Your daily values may be higher or lower depending on your calorie needs.

©www.NutritionData.com

GROCERY SHOPPING: THEN

I never gave much thought to grocery shopping. My mother was responsible for feeding our family and she occasionally gave me a grocery list to pick up items at the corner store. I bought the standard things like eggs, milk, bread, and lunchmeat. When I went to college, I stacked up on pretzels, chips, cookies, popcorn, crackers, peanuts, and other comfort snacks. I guess these sugary foods and the weekly keg of beer contributed to my "Freshman 15."

The college cafeteria provided the three basic meals so I would shop for perishable items that could fit easily into my dormitory fridge. The items had to be small enough to squeeze between the extended family of beer that monopolized the area. I would bet my life that my stomach stored a fat cell that read, "Don't open until Jane's 50th birthday." I am past the half-century mark, so, in the words of Paul Harvey, *now you know the rest of the story*.

GROCERY SHOPPING: NOW

You don't want to shop with this 50 something woman. Grocery shopping has become as much fun as standing topless while having my breast squished between two arctic like, metal plates with the directive to take a deep breath and hold it. Yeah, that's something I look forward to every year. Getting back on topic, I went to a nutritionist and learned how to read the food nutrition labels so I can make healthy food choices. I know how to assess the number of carbohydrates in a specific serving. You do this by subtracting the grams of dietary fiber from the total grams of carbohydrates. Look, you're laughing and learning while reading my candid memoirs. What can I say? I was born to teach.

I now stand in the food aisles, reading each food label like it was an arousing sexual passage from the *Fifty Shades of Grey*. Damn, that E.L. James is one kinky broad. I laughed when I saw a professional woman reading the book while concealing it between the pages of a *Better Homes and Gardens* magazine. Sure, it will make for a *better home* when her husband yanks her hair, pins her to a wall and tongue tickles her tonsils while his erection presses against her belly. Yep, that's sure to get her *garden* swollen. Excuse me, I meant her garden growing. It's not healthy reading James's book while being divorced with the *gotta have a blood test* before having sex with me rule.

Do you see what menopause is doing to me? Healthy foods leading to erotic and impure thoughts? Please don't judge me! The unsettled hormones ripping through my disheveled body bring out the worse in me. It's hard to talk about food after a kaleidoscope of S&M just seduced my mind.

I use to grab a dozen white eggs in the dairy aisle and head home. Now, I only buy brown eggs from the hens that are cage free, are not given any antibiotics or hormones, are fed all natural vegetarian grain with no animal fat or animal by-products and who drink from natural spring waters. The eggs taste delicious because these healthy hens do not spend their days penned up in some tiny, filthy, sunless coop. They are running carefree around the farm basking in the sunshine and laying the freshest brown colored eggs. I know that I will find this awe-inspiring farm somewhere between Peter Pan's *Never Land* and Alice's *Wonderland*.

Back then, milk was milk. It came from a cow. Case closed. Today milk is categorized as whole milk (all milk fat), 2% low fat milk, 1% low fat milk and nonfat milk also known as skim milk. I purchase skim milk exclusively. Why the hell would I want to consume any milk fat at all? Fat? No fat? It's a no brainer. Imagine this declaration coming from a woman who only drank chocolate milk when she was growing up.

I do try to buy the healthiest foods available on the market today. I use to buy foods that were fat free and sugar free but I don't anymore. I read that when the natural fats and sweeteners are removed from foods; it's comparable to a *chemical shit storm* because these foods are being chemically altered to make them taste good. So, what's the real story? Which foods are the healthiest? I'm guessing the answer lies in the Land of Oz, buried in a remote location inside the Wizard's black velvet bag.

DOCTORS THEN

DOCTORS NOW

DOCTORS: THEN

I seldom went to my family doctor. I only made an appointment when I had a severe case of the flu. If my doctor counted on my illnesses to pay back medical school loans, he would have been toast long before the loan giant accepted billions in government bailouts. What's this, Jane being political? I was taught never to discuss religion or politics in large crowds because it only leads to arguments and aggressive behavior. Oh, what the hell, a hostile debate might lead to more business for my family doctor. See, I always find the silver lining.

One doctor that I will never forget is the one who visited our high school three times a year for sports physicals. He was a pleasant elderly man who had to put up with the likes of me. I reminded my friends to wear their skimpiest bras and underwear whenever we had school physicals. Back then, the girls formed a single line and chatted while waiting for the doctor to examine them in the nurse's office. There weren't any partitions and this modest doctor had to deal with a bunch of half-naked noisy teenagers. The school nurse stood next to him, wiping his brow with a small white towel because sweat beads would form on his forehead. I'd give anything to have that 18-year-old body back. If I had a physical under those conditions today, I'd be draped in a painter's tarp while silently waiting my place in line.

DOCTORS: NOW

I have an over-sized calendar that permits me to view the many scheduled doctor appointments that are necessary for my survival. I should take stock in these physicians' practices because I am now paying back their school loans as well as their children's school loans. If you proceed alphabetically, I likely have a doctor representing each of the 26 letters since most entries in my phone book end with MD.

I have my gynecologist or as we in the stirrup world like to say, "My G-man", who takes care of the area that's never discussed with my family doctor. I value my relationship with my primary doctor and I would never compromise that relationship by introducing a vagina or clitoris into the conversation.

Here's a funny story about my G-man. My son was getting married and I went to a tanning salon but not for tanning purposes. I was an island girl who always flaunted a sultry bronze body. I went there to whiten my teeth. That's right, I purchased a whitening kit that was activated by UV rays, and I excitedly rubbed that venomous gel on my choppers. I was stoked (that's a cool word my students use) because I was guaranteed glamorous, movie star quality teeth. The attendant suggested that I might as well tan while lying in the bed. So, I peeled off my clothes but left my bra and panties on. I didn't want those ultraviolet rays burning my fuzzy taco or scorching my areola. Are you girls who fell asleep during health class running a search on areola now? See, you should have paid attention during those high school anatomy lessons. Anyway, I was wearing thin, lacey underwear that revealed intricate designs within the lace. I did my thing in the tanning bed and drove to the mall to buy some last minute particulars for the wedding.

I checked my newly whitened teeth in a dressing room mirror, but noticed a horrible rash around my pubic area. I assumed that I had an allergic reaction to the UV rays or even worse, someone with the "herp" had been in that bed before me and the employee didn't sanitize it properly. I screamed for my friend, who was in the next dressing room, and told her to look at my contaminated rash. She laughed hysterically saying it wasn't a rash just burn marks from the tanning bed's UV rays that outlined the patterns on my lace underwear. Our relationship is similar to the characters, Caroline and Max on the comedy show, **Two Broke Girls.**

I had an appointment with my G-man the following day and I was so embarrassed about the burn marks. I didn't want the doctor thinking I was some twisted, sexual eccentric who enjoyed burning her crotch. I started to explain the uncomfortable situation but my doctor laughed and said there was nothing to be embarrassed about. I learned that other patients purposely brand themselves (mostly with their guys' name) around the crotch and backside areas and request the doctor's opinion in regards to their creative artwork.

My mammary gland reduction required that I have breast X-rays taken at our local hospital. I did as instructed and delivered the film to the plastic surgeon's office on my initial visit. Those boobie pictures had quite the story to tell before being suspended on the surgeon's examination board.

I picked up copies of my X-rays at the hospital and had my three sons with me. My middle son took the film out of the envelope and pressed it against the window of our SUV. Cars were honking and drivers were giving me the thumbs up. I forgot to mention that these were X-rays of double D breasts. I turned around to scold him but the backseat laughter was so contagious that I had to laugh along.

I hid the films behind my bedroom dresser so they would be intact when they reached their destination. My ex-husband and I went out to dinner that evening and my neighbor's daughter watched my children. Again, the mischievous son decided it would be fun to show the babysitter mom's X-rays. He performed Navy Seal maneuvers until the films were discovered in their top secret hiding place.

It was the Christmas season and my boys were eating candy canes while showing the sitter my films. She instructed them to return the envelope to the place they found it and for once, they did as they were told. The sitter told me about the X-ray heist and I just laughed and said that she wasn't the first to see them.

I went to the Plastic Surgeon the following week and handed him my films. He placed one of the sheets on his white board and flipped on the light switch. After fixating on it for an eternity, he turned to me with sad puppy dog eyes. He proceeded to tell me that he is seeing numerous calcium deposits on my X-rays. As he pointed to each one, something was coming off the film and sticking to his finger. He stared at the tiny white particles intently and then proceeded to flick each of the suspected calcium deposits off my X-ray. Turns out, his concerns were nothing more than white pieces of candy cane left there by my meddling sons. I laughed uncontrollably, but, unfortunately, my doctor didn't have my charming sense of humor. As you might have surmised, I ended up having a different plastic surgeon perform my reduction mammoplasty surgery.

MEMORY THEN

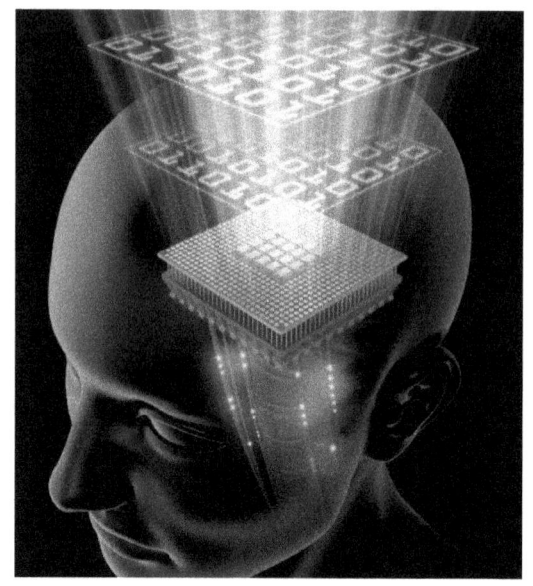

MEMORY NOW

MEMORY: THEN

I had an impressive memory back in the day. I could remember everything I did or needed to do without writing it down. I recalled names, faces, places, dates and any other information that was important to a teenage girl. Classmates referred to my ability as a *photographic memory* because I could literally glance at my textbook and memorize the information on the page. Everyone wanted to be in my learning group because they were guaranteed an *A* on tests and classroom projects. I could repeat everything I saw, heard, tasted, smelled, and touched. Well, there I go again amazing myself. I just realized that I listed the five traditional human senses. See, stored in my brain, somewhere between the alcohol and prescription drugs is a library of information longing to get out.

MEMORY: NOW

Memory? What is a memory? I can't remember what I did today, yesterday, last week, or five minutes ago. Instead of admiring my once impressive memory, my friends get frustrated with my forgetfulness. Believe me, I don't choose to be absentminded. I honestly cannot remember things that are important to my family and friends unless I write them down. The inside of my car is decorated with post-its and my smartphone has an infinite number of listings under the *reminders* icon. I guess nowadays, I am so focused on my worries and obligations that I forget or unconsciously ignore my surroundings. I'm afraid that my forgetfulness will eventually develop into full-blown Alzheimer's but I'm in the *half-heimer* stage at this juncture in life.

Some say that I have a selective memory in that I choose the things that I want to retain. I believe that people, places, and things that were emotional and personal to me are embedded in my long-term memory and will remain there forever. Any other memory is most likely stored on some government hard drive since they know more about me than I know about myself.

You're going to love this *memorable* situation. My younger sister and I look very much alike and many strangers have presumed us twins. One time, after a hectic day of teaching, I ran into the market to pick up a few things for dinner. My mind was all over the place, like a jigsaw puzzle on a card table. I was recalling the day's activities, thinking about the classwork that I had to grade and wondering how dinner and laundry would fit in that night.

I finished shopping and headed for my car. As I was walking, this man approached me and hugged me like he had just found his long lost love. He planted a big kiss on my lips and told me that I looked great. Well, it's not every day that a stranger hugs and kisses me while paying me a compliment. Knowing that I possess the memory of a newborn baby, I figured he was a family friend who I forgot during these menopausal years.

I stared at him as he began talking but I couldn't for the life of me remember him or his face. I'm speculating that he knows me well, since the greeting he gave me wasn't the typical, "Hello." I was watching his lips move but I couldn't hear a sound because my mind was searching the card catalog in my brain for this man's name. When I came out of the fog, he asked me how my children were doing. I told him everyone was well and doing great. The conversation went on for about ten minutes before he mentioned my niece's name. It was then that I realized this man thinks I am my sister. I decided to play him. I told him that I didn't have a daughter and that I didn't appreciate him squeezing me and kissing me on the lips. The guy's eyes grew to the size of golf balls and his face flushed like mine during a hot flash episode. He searched for any kind word he could say in hope that I wouldn't cause a seen.

He introduced himself and humbly explained that there was a woman in town who looked and spoke just like me. I couldn't go all Ashton Kutcher and *punk* him anymore so I told him my sister's name and he started shouting, "Yes, Yes, that's her." We had a good laugh about our complicated conversation. It's funny how I can remember this incident but for the life of me, I can't remember the man or his name.

CAR THEN

CAR NOW

CAR: THEN

I remember how happy I was the day I was taking my driver's road test. It was January 17, 1975, my 17th birthday. I purposely wore a short skirt and a low cut body suit in case I ran over any orange cones when I was parallel parking. I was a Jersey shore girl who didn't need to parallel park. Shore residents park their cars on stone covered driveways that are in the front or on the side of their homes. My family, all eight of us, had one car and dad used it for work. One of my best friend's had a family owned car dealership and her father graciously offered to let me use one of his sports cars for my test. I had never driven the car before and I was nervous to the point of shaking. I didn't have any Xanax back then, just my seductive schoolgirl clothing. Turns out, that's all I needed. The officer who proctored my road test must have dug (cool old school word) my outfit because from the minute he jumped into my borrowed car, he stared at me and continued to stare at me throughout the entire test. Best of all, he never made me parallel park. Well, I got my license but didn't have a car to drive. My friends let me drive their cars occasionally and my boyfriend had a white Trans Am that he shared with me. Still, I wanted my own car so bad.

When I went to college, my friend, roommate and partner in crime drove a tan Rambler that we christened, "the swiss cheese mobile." That car had more holes in it than George Zimmerman's courtroom testimony but it was reliable and always got us to where we needed to go. My roommate's family was moving from New Jersey to Florida and her parents decided to get rid of the car because it wasn't worth transporting. They agreed to sell it to me for a dollar because that was the minimum amount required to transfer the car title.

I was flying on air. Jane was now the proud owner of a swiss cheese tan Rambler. I didn't care what it looked like because my friend and I cherished the many great memories made in that car and I was going to make some more. I had the car for a week and decided to drive home to show off my new ride. Everyone had a good laugh when they saw my car's battle scars but they were happy that I finally had wheels of my own.

The drive back to school, that Monday morning, was about a two-hour ride and I left my house around 6:00am. I proudly belted myself into the driver's seat and headed up the Garden State Parkway. I wasn't a half hour into the drive when I heard banging sounds coming from under my car. The sounds were intensifying and when I looked in the rear view mirror, I could see metal scattered all over the road. The steering wheel started shaking violently yet I managed to guide the car off to the shoulder of the road. My memories were now scraps of steel and iron haphazardly distributed over the northbound lane of the parkway. I gazed in disbelief and started to cry.

A car filled with men in their 20's pulled up behind me. Three of them exited the car and approached me as I stood there crying and holding my duffle bag that carted my clean clothes from home. I remember being terrified. It was early morning and I didn't have a cell phone in the 70's. Cars were whizzing by on their way to work or they were heading home from a weekend at the Jersey shore. Nobody stopped to help the damsel in distress. Monday morning on the Garden State Parkway is comparable to the Running of the Bulls in Mexico and it's every man for himself.

One of the guys abruptly informed me that since I didn't need my gas, he and his friends were going to syphon it from my car. Another one rudely interrupted and told me that the casino had taken all their money and they didn't have enough gas to make it home. These guys most likely lost their money in some back alley brothel, not at a casino gaming table in Atlantic City. The third guy carried a case of empty beer bottles with tubing that apparently came from Tony Soprano's basement. I decided to let them have the gas without any questions or inquiries. I certainly didn't want to be "tubed up" and thrown into the wooded area off the parkway.

The guy carrying the case of bottles lay on the ground and sucked the life out of my gas tank. Looking back, I'm wondering if he ever did porn. STOP, Jane. Pornography has no relevance to this story. There, I just disciplined myself. Like that's normal. Nonetheless, the dirt bag filled each bottle with my fuel, and then ran to pour the gas into his tank. I asked the assholes to notify the state police to my whereabouts but one of them sarcastically said, "Yeah, like that's going to happen." Seems the Dukes of Hazard boys wanted to get a head start on the law.

About an hour later, a state police car pulled over. The officer radioed his dispatcher and instructed her to call my dad, who thankfully hadn't left for work. As I drove away in my father's car, cheeks pinned against the back seat window, I waved good-bye to my gasless, engineless car.

CAR: NOW

I bet you're eagerly anticipating reading about my Hummer, Jaguar, Porsche or BMW. Well, you're enthusiasm just veered to disbelief. You're thinking that a chick (is that word used anymore) with my wit and attitude must drive some bitching car. It's a bitch of a car all right. I drive a 2001, 4-door sedan that humbly parades its scrapes, scratches, dents and battle scars across the roads and highways. This is what happens to a hard working woman who gives her heart and soul to family and career. She turns around to discover that she owes more than she's worth. I have tears right now because sometimes life can really suck.

The 2001 silver automobile is safe and reliable. I thank my lucky stars for the skillful and honest mechanic who maintains the integrity of my timeworn car. This man gets me to where I need to go. That reminds me of something I use to write whenever one of my students' received their driving license. I would write, "I hope your steering wheel takes you to the places your heart wants to go." I am tearing up again, but these are happy tears because I can still see the pride in those teenagers' eyes when they proudly showed me their ticket to freedom.

Who knows, maybe one day when I become a famous writer, my silver, 2001, 4-door sedan will be parked in the Smithsonian Natural Museum of American History next to

Archie Bunker's tan upholstered chair. A girl can dream, can't she? A dream is a wish that stays with you, year after year, through each blown out candle on your birthday cake.

BAR SCENE THEN

BAR SCENE NOW

BAR SCENE: THEN

Summers at the Jersey shore were the best, especially when the legal drinking age was 18. I would finish waitressing at the Pancake House around 2:00 and then head to the beach with my friends to swim, tan, and meet up with the guys. We'd head home when it started getting dark to nap and get ready for an always-entertaining night at the local bars.

Our nights typically started around 11:00 and ended when the bartender alerted the drinkers to *last call*. We patronized the bars later in the evening to eliminate the possibility of running into seniors dancing to the Twist, Stroll, or Bunny Hop. The 18-25 year old crowd labeled anyone over 30 a senior citizen

My boyfriend didn't dance and he never liked it when I danced or if a guy tried to dance with me. His attitude caused many uncomfortable altercations that usually resulted in trash talk or some tourist being tossed around the bar. I think I have a form of Attention Deficit Disorder or ADD when it comes to dancing. When the music starts, I start and I don't stop dancing until the band or DJ calls it a night. I am a dance-a-holic.

My dancing almost ended our relationship, which did end some 29 years later. We were out with a bunch of friends, at one of our favorite bars, and the band was awesome. I was in a zone and I had the music in me. The lead singer announced a dance contest in which the winner would receive prizes. He continued to say that he needed 10 female contestants. One of the band members pointed to me and motioned for me to come on stage. I was standing next to him before his arm went down. The other nine contenders came forward like silly schoolgirls. I was in it to win it. After all, there were prizes to be won. I saw my disgruntled boyfriend make a move to the stage but the bouncers were on him like Anthony Weiner on his cell phone.

The band's drummer began broadcasting the rules of the dance competition. The winner would be declared the *Rock Queen* if she could wiggle her mid-section in a fashion similar to Elvis Presley as he gyrated to *Hound Dog* on the Milton Berle Show. The drummer would tell each girl how many times he was going to strike the drum and that's the number of times she would *rock* back and forth and around in a circle. The audience's applause would decide the winner. Some sheepish girls rocked 10 to15 times but my number was an astounding 50. I proudly did my Elvis interpretation and the crowd went wild. I was wearing a pair of white hot pants and a half top so I'm sure my outfit enhanced my dance appeal. When I finished my 50 *rocks,* I glanced in my boyfriend's direction and noticed that he was heading towards the door. I didn't care, I was the *Rock Queen* and I was about to be awarded my prizes. The bartender handed the singer a flimsy paper sash, doused with red glitter that read, **ROCK QUEEN**. He positioned the sash across my chest and swung my right arm into the air. He announced that I had won the drink of my choice. The partygoers gave me a standing ovation but I wanted to go all Sissy Spacek on them and unleash *Carrie's* telekinetic fury on this band and bartender. Imagine, 50 hard rocks and all I got was a paper sash and a fucking drink? I tore off the sash and headed home. It was near closing time anyway. The story doesn't end there.

The next morning, I went to work at the Pancake House. Two handsome surfer type guys were whispering while staring at me. When I approached their table, I saw a 20-dollar bill in front of each of them. The one surfer told me that if I answered a yes or no question, he would give me 20 dollars. I figured, what the hell, how tough could the question be? Well, get this, he asked me if I was the **ROCK QUEEN** from last night. I wanted the money, so I replied, "Yes". He jumped from his seat, high fived me and handed me the twenty. The other guy muttered, "Shit", and shook his head. I figured my identity was questionable since the morning after look isn't exactly flattering. I snickered when I realized that some of the red glitter was still on my hand. Maybe that gave the winner the clue he needed!

BAR SCENE: NOW

A wild night out for my 50 something friends is being able to purchase half price drinks and half price appetizers between the hours of four and seven. Their alternative is patronizing a BYOB restaurant that offers early bird specials. The sad thing is that I'm becoming one of them. Don't get me wrong, I can still party, but the *last call for alcohol* only happens once or twice a year. Like Cinderella, my bewitching hour seems to be the stroke of twelve since the baby boomer generation knows *nothing good happens in a bar after midnight*.

I was in a pub with my BFF's and we were having a wonderful time drinking, laughing, and reminiscing about the good old days. Classic rock and roll was resonating in the background as the hours and minutes faded away. Bruce Springsteen's *Glory Days* abruptly stopped and a deafening noise took over the tavern. We couldn't hear each other's words anymore. The bar's front doors swung open and people with gauges, piercings, body tattoos, and purple and blue hair besieged our happy place. We exited the bar quicker than OJ Simpson fleeing in his white Ford Bronco. We laughed when we reached the parking lot and decided to continue our conversation at the diner up the street. This is the reason we can't make *last call* any longer. We're old...Damn it...We're old.

I know that I still have the music in me but it's stuck somewhere between the extra pounds and a barrel of wine. I can't believe wine is my go to alcohol these days. Old school Jane threw back beer and whiskey. Toby Keith would have loved this *little whiskey girl*. He's my favorite country singer and if I'm in a bar that still has a jukebox, my first selection is Toby's, *I Love This Bar*. If I'd mentioned country music 35 years ago, my popularity would have sunk to the levels of Tiger Woods and Paris Hilton.

I recently rejuvenated my archaic body and spent 12 hours drinking and partying in Nashville, TN. The grandeur of Lower Broadway with row after row of honky-tonk bars conjured up a down and dirty cowgirl from the likes of this Yankee Doodle girl. It's the magic of Nashville that captures the essence of hopeful and hungry musicians whose dreams of wealth and fame are alive in their voices and guitars day after day. They sing and sweat to mobs of adoring fans and their audience friendly performances encourage crowd participation.

I was on the first level of a three-story bar and a young girl was singing a beautiful country ballad. I heard dance music bellowing from the second floor and I raced up a level of stairs. I stood in the doorway feeling footloose and fancy-free. Southern rock was blasting through the speakers as I made my way to the center of the room. I leaped on stage with the ease of an Olympic hurdler. I started singing with the band and circling the guitarist as if he were a pole dancer's prop. The horde of people began hooting and hollering for more. So, I gave them more. I do this dance where I raise my right arm over my head, bend my knees, touch my hand to the floor, and slowly stand up as my hand seductively moves up my body and over my head once more. Let me tell you, this move is a real crowd pleaser.

I glanced around and saw a sea of iPhones and cameras pointed in my direction. Not to worry, I had 6 hours of drinking under my belt and my teaching days were over. I danced with the band through two more songs, and then exited the stage with an open invitation to rejoin the group that evening for their 11:00 performance. People began approaching me and asking me if I was part of the band. I smiled awkwardly because my 55 year old body was breathless from all the singing and dancing. A few suggested that the band hire me because I stole the show. I wanted to say, "Thank you", but my chest was heaving in and out and my heart was pounding like Julia Child's mallet against a side of beef.

A 30 something guy walked over with a girl and handed me a beer. He told me it was well deserved and that he and his wife really enjoyed my performance. She spoke up and told me that I had great legs and if her legs looked that good at 45, she would be a happy woman. I loved that girl. She had just erased 10 years from my biological clock. I must admit, I did look hot that day with my short lace skirt, off the shoulder country blouse and cowgirl boots and hat.

Late that evening, I stormed the stage at yet another honky-tonk bar but it was a much younger crowd. You remember those hair-raising late night people. The band was very accommodating and one fellow (that's an old person's word) handed me a microphone. I sang and danced to a round of applause but this time it felt different.

A young guy moved towards the stage, looked in my direction, and yelled, "This is for you". He tossed up about 20 singles and blew me a kiss. Voices from the crowd encouraged me to pick up the money but I waited until the end of the song and skillfully made my way to the back of the room. It was cool to have my 15 minutes of fame but it wasn't cool feeling like an old stripper dancing for some unsolicited dollar bills. When I reenacted this story for my friends, they said I was crazy for not taking the money. The party girls considered it payment for another two drinks. My time in Nashville was definitely one for the memory books.

TELEVISION THEN

TELEVISION NOW

TELEVISION: THEN

Our family television was a piece of furniture that complemented the scheme of our Early American living room set. I dusted and polished that wooden square box every Saturday morning. Family photographs rested proudly on top of the television as well as an antenna dubbed *rabbit ears*. I remember jiggling those metal wires while my father hollered, "Stop right there." I would stop right there but the fuzziness in the TV set would return and I would begin the ritual again.

I didn't watch much television when I was young because there were eight family members and just one TV. Dad controlled the television set when he wasn't working so there were countless hours of college and professional sports being transmitted into our home. My father was a sports junkie and he knew more about sports than did the athletes themselves.

We did have family time watching television shows that we could all enjoy. Shows like *Happy Days, The Brady Bunch, Let's Make a Deal, The Price is Right*, and *The Walton's* to name a few. One of my fondest memories was watching the *Miss America Pageant* with my family. We tried to predict the top 10 contestants, the top three finalists, and the new Miss America.

In colleges, class schedules were built around the soap opera, *General Hospital*. Students couldn't wait to watch the on and off romantic relationship between super couple Luke Spencer and Laura Webber. College campuses put the show on television's daytime map. The popular soap was a campus craze as well as a teenage rage. The future generation for the greatness nation on earth, was glued to ABC's General Hospital as they watched a drunken Luke forcing himself on Laura, on the campus disco floor while Herb Alpert's song, *Rise* played in the background. ABC portrayed the incident as a seduction instead of a rape because Laura eventually fell in love and married her assailant. Whatever the show's attraction, even mega-star Elizabeth Taylor was smitten and intrigued by the adventures of Luke and Laura. She called producer Gloria Monty and requested a cameo role on the show. I guess she felt compelled to provide on set marriage counseling for Luke and Laura after her six failed marriages. Taylor appeared on five episodes of General Hospital as a vindictive widow. And that my friend is yet another teaching moment courtesy of Jane.

TELEVISION: NOW

I watch sitcoms, reality singing competitions, cable and network news, and NFL games. I don't know how I arrived at this crossroad in life but any type of horror, crime drama, hospital drama or shows with rampant violence are not entertaining to me. In fact, they are upsetting and worrisome. Before turning 50, I could watch any genre of television. Maybe it's age, hormones, or some other mid-life intrusion that intuitively restricts my television boundaries. The other night, I was channel surfing and came across a show that my sons' rave about so I decided to check it out and see what the excitement was all about. I saw masked men standing over a baby's crib while a mother pleaded for her child's life. One man ruthlessly threatened the woman as she stood frozen in time. My heart palpitated, my hands grew clammy, my internal temperatures seared, and I screamed, "Leave that baby alone." The grandmother in me instinctively needed to protect the child and wreak havoc on those thugs by smashing the television screen and climbing into that baby's bedroom. I knew this was a disturbing reaction so I turned the television off and read a book. If ever a Xanax was warranted, it was now.

Sitcoms chill me out and allow me to escape from the real world even if it's for half an hour. I don't have to engage in any thought provoking processes. I just laugh at the characters that I can identify with because their lives are normally more screwed up than mine, making me seem normal. Kudos to the actors because making me seem normal isn't an easy thing to do. I appreciate happy endings (get your mind out of the gutter), loving relationships and the trust and loyalty between characters. Situation comedies allow me to accept my strengths and weaknesses by laughing at jokes about everyday life that truthfully are just jokes about me.

Reality singing competition shows bring out the singer in me. You know, the girl who dreams of becoming a Pop Diva and sees her over five decades age as months of musical expertise noted on her resume. The number represents the countless, dedicated years of singing experience. The down side is the only singing experience I've had is in my house, in my car, and in my classroom. Some students appreciated my singing while others told me not to quit my daytime job.

That's because they loved me and didn't want me to leave teaching for a life on the big stage. Sounds reasonable, right? Occasionally, I perform karaoke in front of an intoxicated bar crowd and I get the normal round of applause. My brother hinted that they were clapping because I was finished singing my song. I just chalk the comment up to sibling jealousy and we'll leave it at that.

It makes my heart happy to see contestants who make it big, especially those who are down on their luck or stuck in a dead-end job. It's cool to follow their music careers throughout the years. A student once told me that if you use the word *cool*, you aren't. You're just old. If the shoe fits….If you completed that phrase, you're old too. Gotcha.

I watch cable and network news so I can stay informed about local, national, and world events. The news is so depressing and I find myself feeling sad, confused, and sometimes afraid after watching and listening to it. I'm not in favor of reporters identifying a person who has committed a horrific crime. This allows the suspect the attention he/she desires even if the story presents itself in a notorious way. Just report the incident but don't mention names. I'm not a psychiatrist but making criminals anonymous and denying them the publicity they crave might reduce the number of atrocities in this country. Just saying.

 After watching the news last night, I reached the conclusion that I base my television restrictions on the hostile happenings in this fast and ever changing world. Terrorism, murder, death, horrific graphic imagery, fear, crime, hatred, and sadness make me feel worse than menopause. It appears that nothing positive is happening in our world. News is a definite downer.

A happy makes your heart feel good newsmagazine program can be viewed on Sunday mornings. The show's thematic logo is a distinguishing sun that appears in a variety of forms throughout the 90-minute program. The suns' changing faces reflect the aura and mood of individual story segments. I appreciate the human-interest stories that get lost on network and cable news. The program's slow pace and quiet tone provides the viewing audience a laissez-faire persona as they sip their coffee or tea and in some cases, a mimosa, Bloody Mary or *hair of the dog*. A hair of the dog is a cocktail consumed by partygoers experiencing alcohol withdrawal symptoms from their, "I can't remember anything about Saturday night." Its goal is to minimize the effects of a banging hangover. What the hell is wrong with me? I take something as beautiful as a face in the sun and turn it into a drinker's dictionary. Now, back to the feel good newsmagazine program.

Each week the show concludes with a 60-second tranquil nature scene accompanied by a soothing trumpet melody. This peaceful moment in time is important to me, especially during football season when my inner beast is released once the games begin.

I love NFL football. Some people can't understand how I can stay inside, on a beautiful Fall day, and watch football. One family member described the game as a bunch of grown men falling down and getting back up again. I must admit, that's funny stuff. I miss watching the games with my Dad because he gave me so much insight and behind the scenes information about the NFL. We cheered and jeered for our favorite team and I cherish those times together.

One of the highlights of NFL football, besides the drinking, is the friendly banter between me and the opposing team's fans on Facebook. My iPhone is within an arm's reach and the minute anything text worthy happens, my fingers start tapping away. I enjoy sending humorous photographs that trash players and teams because it really gets people fired up. Be assured, it's all done in good fun. I would love to know the number of posts Facebook records throughout the football season.

During Sunday games, I eat, drink, and sit in a reclining chair throughout the day. I don't want to get football spread (similar to the wide ass secretary spread) so I decided this year to become a cheerleader. I have team jerseys, white and black skirts, pom-poms and some badass dance moves. I cheer when the spirits move me. These spirits comprise the supernatural as well as those shrouded in my beer, wine, and vodka. My friend videotaped some of my cheers and I shared them on FB. I was pleasantly surprised to see the number of positive comments and numerous hits on the *Like* button. I am extremely grateful that FB does not offer a *Dislike* button.

GIRL TALK THEN

GIRL TALK NOW

GIRL TALK: THEN

Oh, to be young again. I miss those high school and college days when I chatted with my friends about things that were important to us. We were in such a rush to grow up, be independent and live life on our terms. We achieved one milestone after another and kept pushing for freedom and independence. We wanted to hurry up time. Little did we know, time was flying bye.

Monday was a bragging rights day where we embellished the weekend's events. Human ears became elephant ears while listening to juicy gossip about guys and sex. Periodically a movie or concert received attention but in between guys and sex. Cramps and menstrual issues somehow always seemed to surface. Locker talk occasionally became scandalous if someone admitted to dating another girl's ex. That scenario was unfathomable in *girl talk* world.

Believe me; the bragging rights did not stop at the girls' lockers. Boasting Don Juans held court in the boys' locker rooms telling tales of sex with unsuspecting girls. One creep crowed about having sex with me and all I did was kiss him because he bought me a record album and I felt obligated. I guess his idea of reaching first base was a lot different from mine. Isn't that ridiculous, boys linking sex to baseball? That would be like girls coupling sex with makeup. Let's compare the two.

1. (first base) Kissing = eyeliner
2. (second base) Fondling = mascara
3. (third base) Oral Pleasure= lipstick
4. (home plate) Intercourse= blush

I must admit, my makeup and sex association was brilliant. Maybe juvenile, but brilliant nonetheless.

Tuesday's and Wednesday's girl talk focused on sports (girls playing sports or watching their boyfriends participating in sports), trashing and criticizing teachers over tests and homework, comparing after school meeting times and complaining about the jocks, nerds, kiss-asses and stoners in class. Boys, sex and menstrual cramps were referenced too.

Thursday's dialog fixated on family responsibilities, parents' ridiculous expectations and demands, new movie listings, impending rock concerts, weekend social activities, and weight gain courtesy of the cafeteria food. Also addressed were boys, sex, and a girl's *monthly friend*.

Friday's conversations were the best. Excitement filled the air whenever word trickled out that someone's parents decided to take a Saturday night hiatus from their pompous teen. The news started a chain reaction of invites, party plans, and ready to deliver alibies for inquiring moms and dads. Girls begged other girls to hook them up while others pleaded to borrow jeans and sensuous shirts. Mobs of students attended Friday night basketball games and Saturday afternoon football games so Friday's lunch chitchat focused on feasible bleacher seat shenanigans. Guys, sex, and menstrual cramps always managed to resurface in female conversations. Overall, Friday talk usually pertained to the up-and-coming weekend with promises of adventure, fun, hallmark memories, and love.

Did you notice the common denominators involving *girl talk then*? There you have it, guys, sex, and menstrual cramps. A foreshadowing of advice, these three topics will not play an important role later in life.

Looking back, it's funny how teenagers perceive high school and college graduations as highlights and highpoints in life. In reality, graduation is simply an end to some of the best live adolescent footage ever made…..yours and mine.

One of my favorite songs about the coming of age is Trace Adkins' **You're Gonna Miss This.** Trace urges teenagers to cherish innocence, and to slow life down. He sings:

"You're gonna miss this
You're gonna want this back
You're gonna wish these days hadn't gone by so fast
These Are Some Good Times
So take a good look around
You may not know it now
But you're gonna miss this"

You know something, Trace, I really do miss those days.
I would give anything to have them back.
Especially knowing what I know now.

GIRL TALK: NOW
Do you remember the three common denominators involved in *girl talk then*? Well, I do and I don't give a rat's ass about guys, sex, and menstrual cramps. Do you want to know why? It's because I don't have them anymore. My menstrual period stopped years ago, my sex life is insignificant after mandating blood testing for potential

suitors and there's no need to talk about men if you're not having sex with them. Well, some of my 50 something friends still talk about sex but not in a good way.

My friends are the best thing that's ever happened to me with the exception of my three incredible sons and my beautiful grandson. Therefore, I guess they're not the best things that ever happened to me. However, they're damn close.

Midlife girl talk fluctuates from children to medical to sexual to alcohol to medications to work to the ridiculous to pets to….You get the point. Menopausal women's conversations can drift from topic to topic in the time it takes to blink an eye. My friend came to visit the other day and I hadn't seen her in a few months. She started to tell me something important, but I cut her off mid-sentence because one word she spoke made me think of something else. She replied, "Jane, let me finish this thought because if I don't we won't get back to it for at least two hours." I let her finish her thought, but by then, I had forgotten mine.

Meal conversations go against everything I taught my children. Specifically never to bring up nauseating topics while eating because it can sicken people and make them lose their appetite.

For whatever reason, urinary problems multiply whenever older women get together, especially if women in the group have three or more children. It seems those precious bundles of joy stored in our pelvic cavity for nine months, caused our uterus to press against our now oversized bladders resulting in leakage, urgent and frequent urination, involuntary urination, urinary retention and finally anxiety over all of these urinary concerns. That's enough to skip a meal, right? Hell no. We mid-lifers have become so accustomed to this kind of talk that we eat more because we're feeling so depressed.

Pets are another story. I don't have a pet and I don't dislike animals except when their noses are up my crotch and they're dry-humping my leg. It's particularly disturbing when they're dressed better than many middle class children are. I went to a baby shower with friends I've known for over 20 years. At our table were a mother and her adult daughter who we just met. My one friend yammered on about her baby, Bella. She boasted how cute Bella looked in her new cheerleading outfit and that she had taken her to a professional photographer. She took out her wallet and showed the group Bella's cheerleading picture. The woman and daughter's reactions were priceless. They gasped when glancing at the Maltese. The conversation quickly switched to the baby shower game in progress. I guess an hour had elapsed since Bella's photograph was shown. The talk now focused on children and my friend with the dog said that she couldn't wait to have grandchildren. Our *new* friend spoke up and said, "You have your granddaughter, Bella." I spit my wine out and nearly peed my pants (remember the over active bladder) from laughing so hard. After realizing it was a dog's photograph, the woman admitted that she thought the baby had a different look. Well duh, she's a dog. I told my friend to give Bella a damn bone and leave the fashion industry to the humans.

Sex is hysterical with the older crowd. Our lunch group had a humorous discussion. The married women complained that Viagra ruined sexual spontaneity and by the time their man's floppy disk became a hard drive, the docking station wasn't interested anymore. Others compared sex to a chore that they didn't feel like doing. I spoke up and suggested that the grass isn't always greener on the other side. I explained the feeling of emptiness and loneliness when sleeping alone. One colleague blurted out, "You want a man? You can borrow mine for the weekend. He had blood work recently and he's fine." Others followed suit in prostituting their husbands. I actually considered the offer knowing that I wouldn't die from a sexually transmitted disease but then common sense reeled me in. After all, we've all learned that you don't defecate where you work.

Medical issues that get the most attention in seniorville are high blood pressure and insomnia. Some causes of hypertension are obesity and consuming more than one alcoholic drink a day. In my defense, I am still losing baby weight from my almost 10-pound son. Granted he's 25 years old, but ask any mother and they'll affirm that dropping baby fat is not an easy thing to do. Just don't summon those overzealous gym rats since they'll tell you they were wearing a bikini two months after giving birth. I *effing* hate them.

What's this about alcohol? Consuming more than one alcoholic beverage a day can lead to high blood pressure? That's like saying you can only have one kernel of popcorn from the bowl or one peanut from the jar. Sipping cocktails with friends is as common as breathing oxygen. I don't drink on a daily basis but I do drink every other day since I retired from teaching. My younger sister wants me to write one of my memoirs for this book under the influence of wine. She thinks I'll be funnier if I have an edge. You know something; I think I'd be good friends with Kathy Lee and Hoda. Those early morning partiers seem to savor their fish bowl glasses of wine even though they are more sippers than drinkers. If my friends and I hosted that show, there would be bleeps and black outs throughout most of the program. We're more like the female versions of Anthony Bourdain.

So many of my female friends have sleep issues. It's no wonder why. We juggle an infinite list of responsibilities and stretch ourselves to the breaking point. We experience all of life's stressors and worry about our health, family, children, jobs, money, marriage, divorce, and life in general. I am tired of people telling me not to sweat the small stuff. In a woman's eyes, no problem is ever too small.

I had insomnia so bad before, during, and after my divorce that the bags under my eyes could carry groceries. I lay awake night after night staring at the bedroom ceiling as a kaleidoscope of uncertainties overwhelmed my brain. I went to my Doctor looking like a cast member from the *Walking Dead*. He prescribed a sleeping pill that allowed me to sleep like a baby until I started having vivid nightmares that woke me up in tears. I even sent out an email, late at night, to everyone at school soliciting donations for BINGO. I job coached one of my students after school, at a nursing home, and the prize cart needed some contributions. I had no idea that I even composed an email until the following morning when I arrived at school. My principal hollered, "Hey Hall, don't you sleep, that email you sent out last night woke me up."

I ran to my computer to inspect the email. I was relieved to read its contents since the subject matter could have been extremely unprofessional. Thankfully, I was thinking about BINGO prizes and not sex or some other potentially embarrassing topic that might have left me on the unemployment line. I could have been soliciting a lot more than BNGO prizes. I am proud to say that I am weaning off sleeping pills but it's not an easy road.

One ridiculous conversation is winning the lottery. The Executive Director of the American Statistical Association stated that a player buying a single ticket has about a 1 in 175 million chance of winning the Powerball Lottery. That's probably a little less than my chances of having a man take a blood test for a sexually transmitted disease. Whenever we talk about the lottery, we promise to share our winnings with one another. It's like me saying that my one wish in life is for me to be fat and my friends to be skinny. However, sharing with friends is nice so we continue the charade.

I went out with three of my best friends, one Saturday night, in search of future husbands or someone willing to buy us a couple drinks. One girl is married but she tags along so she can remind us of our foolish behavior the following morning. I say us, but it's usually just me. Before reaching the bar, we stopped for some scratch off lottery tickets that promised the winner 1,000 dollars a week for life. We bought four tickets and anxiously scratched them off while in the car. One friend, who's the Ryan Seacrest host of lottery games, made us swear that if we hit the big prize we'd share the weekly winnings. There was silence in the car.

Now, hitting the Powerball and promising to share is one thing, but a thousand a week for life and sharing, well, that's another thing. Let's figure, 1,000 dollars split four ways is 250 dollars a week and then with taxes, well, for me it's just not happening. We all reluctantly agreed to the terms but knowing without a court order, the verbal promise wasn't worth an ice cube in hell. The scratching frenzy continued for 20 minutes because every time we'd rub off numbers, somebody would win enough to buy another card or two. When the final card was tossed aside, silver metallic shavings were everywhere. Contagious laughter filled the car because it looked like New Year's Eve had hurled on us. The only winner in that vehicle was my friend who ran in and out of the convenience store five times to retrieve the gaming cards. The calories she burned off were equivalent to a 12-ounce bottle of lite beer.

We moseyed into the bar like the wolf pack in the movie, *Hangover*. We expected all eyes to turn to us, but to our dismay, all eyes stayed glued to their significant other. It sucks going out on Saturday night because it's date night. Damn those online social sites, they really weaken the community dating pool. We traveled to three different bars in search of fun but fun wasn't out that night.

Unfortunately, the only thing we brought home were silvery remnants of our scratch off lottery cards. We may have lost at the game of chance and the game of love, but we'll always be winners in the BFF game. For those of you living under a rock, that stands for *Best Friends Forever.*

Another silly exchange is pondering the dark question of shaving or not shaving the vulva area. In street lingo, should I mow the lawn or keep some grass on the field? Debates, discussions, and giggles about a bikini wax, a Brazilian wax, or a landing strip trim accompany a happy hour attitude. My single friends advised me that guys prefer very little hair down there. They respect women's feelings regarding *beard burn* by shaving their faces every day so guys would appreciate the girls returning the favor by keeping *the clam* seaweed free.

Really, a bikini wax or a Brazilian wax? Not many women over 50 are donning a bikini unless they've been under a surgeon's knife so a waxed pubic area is no excuse for unsightly stretch marks and saddle bag skin. Ladies, let's keep things tidy by using quality razors that offer a stubble-free camel toe shave. The only things touching down on my landing strip these days are a washcloth and a bar of soap. I don't need graphic imagery outlining my vagina so some pilot can position his cockpit in my flight data box. My honey pot is as smooth as a baby's face, not as bushy as a beaver's behind.

UNDERGARMENTS THEN

UNDERGARMENTS NOW

UNDERGARMENTS: THEN

Undergarments were simple back then. I wore cotton bikini underwear and cotton bras. I had that soft downy fiber obsession going on and cotton allowed things *up there* and *down there* to breathe. Cotton carries perspiration away quickly and provides greater circulation allowing fewer irritations in the most sensitive of areas. This was important to a female athlete who sweated profusely during games and practices. I don't recall who said this, but I remember the one constant being that the crotch of my underwear needed to be cotton.

 I could wear nylon, satin or lace panties as long as the crotch was cotton. Am I making myself clear about the cotton crotch? Do you want inflammation or a possible yeast infection? I'm sorry about the bitchiness but I haven't been feeling well the past few days, paired with the thought of going for my mammogram tomorrow morning. I can't wait to have some woman yanking on the twins and pretending she's not checking them out.

I remember those immature boobie comments made by boys that contributed to their stupidity. One being, "It must be foggy out, your *high beams* are on" or "Looks like you're a bit *nippy* today," and "Why did you buy a bra when *I'd hold them up for free*?" Finally, the classic line, "You know, Jane, you're my *breast friend*."

As a young woman, I always wanted to look sexy for my man, but purchasing expensive lingerie was just a waste of money. The lingerie spent more time on the floor than it did on me. Men are in their sexual prime at 18 and their primal brain instinctively tells their testicles to discharge a round of testosterone that could rip through any nylon, satin, or lace panty barricade. They are interested in doing the nasty; not looking at the pretty. I want to surrender the STD blood test requirement right now because my menopausal hormones are on a *catch and release* course. Catch some guy for a quickie and then release him before any personal or emotional attachment develops. The good news is that I haven't lost my sexual libido. The bad news is that I'm all talk, still just a scaredy cat.

UNDERGARMENTS: NOW

Oh, just the thought of buying undergarments makes me wish I were at the dentist having a tooth extracted or at the gynecologist having a vaginal biopsy. It's comparable to purchasing a bathing suit and you know how much I cherish that assignment. I always wore a perfect 36C but after my first child, I jumped to a 40DD. The soft cotton bras of long ago made way for big, bulky, underwire bras with four and five-hook closures.

The incident that traumatized me into pursuing a breast reduction, besides the fact that I walked like the hunchback of Notre Dame, was a day of bra shopping at the mall with my younger sister and her friend. My boobs were massive mammary glands and I felt like a fishing line anchored to the ocean floor. I grabbed a bra in a box, and self-consciously entered the women's dressing room. I requested my sister's opinion regarding the latex contraption as her friend turned and let out a terrifying gasp that drew the attention of everyone within a two-mile radius. The five-hook enclosure on the double D's stunned the A cup lassie and she couldn't control her shock. I did not purchase the bra or any other bra that day; I dressed quietly and fled the intimate apparel department never to return.

 After the breast reduction, I excitedly ran out and bought a 36 C sexy black bra. Tears of disappointment spoiled my enthusiasm for the new lingerie as it slid off my shoulders, crept up my breasts, and exposed fat that spilled over the sides and back of the bra. Intimate apparel manufacturers must use cutout paper dolls for bra models because bras these days tend to be more skimpy than size appropriate. If I really want a bra that's both practical and sexy, I might as well use decorative duct tape and wrap it around my aging girls to get that firm, uplifting look. You never know, it might become a fashion trend for the mature crowd. The slogan could be, **Duct It All**.

My underwear of choice is the cotton high leg brief offered in a multitude of colors at a reasonable five for $26.00. I purchase them in the store that holds a woman's secret. The panties wash beautifully and last a long time. I know young girls red flag the high leg briefs as certifiable granny panties but, hey, I buy them from a sexy lingerie shop so that should qualify me as dope or sick (teens use those last two words to mean awesome).

One of my favorite high school students left a note on my desk that read, "You're the shit." I felt faint when another student noticed my distress and told me the writing meant, "You're the coolest." I didn't believe him so I investigated its meaning in the *Urban Dictionary* and discovered that he was telling the truth. If you want to find the connotation of unfamiliar words and phrases used by young people, search the *Urban Dictionary*, a web based dictionary that offers a bounty of streetwise lingo. Glad I could help break the generational language barrier. You're welcome.

What's up with thongs? Did a 300-pound man, wearing knee-highs and a cock sock market them? Do you think I'm joking? Run an internet search on *cock sock* and you'll see the male answer to the female thong. It's the modern day Tarzan's loincloth. I'll take old school Tarzan any day.

Thongs might be sexy but I can't wear anything that's flosses my butt crack and gives me a permanent wedgie. I realize women worry about panty lines but do they worry about exposing their cauliflower asses to a disenchanted public? It's just gross and unsanitary. The over 55 crowd can remember the revolting sanitary napkin belts worn before the stick-on maxi and mini pads, so why in hell would they ever want to wear a thong?

 Thongs conjure up embarrassing and uncomfortable flashbacks from my elementary school years of wearing what seemed to be a thick rubber band around my waist. Attached to the rubber band were two elastic straps that had the appearance of white paper clips. The paper clips cradled a cotton cloth between my legs that repositioned itself every time I moved. There you have it, these disturbing memories are enough to make me rush out and buy some sexy thong underwear...NOT.

As far as functional lingerie, Spanx has my vote of confidence. I never heard the word SPANX until my younger sister and I almost ruined our niece's wedding. My niece lives in Philadelphia so we drove up from the Jersey Shore to visit a bridal shop in the city. The place was bustling with future brides and their wedding parties. My sister and I wanted to emphasize our voluptuous breast but the other girls didn't have much going on up north so what we liked, they didn't and vice versa. We searched through an endless collection of dresses until we finally agreed on a two-piece sky blue gown. It was an agonizing process trying on gown after gown but the cocktails that followed made it worth our efforts. I love being part of an Irish family.

We were one of the last bridal parties in the shop and the seamstress was fatigued after a harrowing day of taping, and pinning. She had no idea who or what she was measuring. Order forms flew everywhere as she fondled, fastened, and spun us around like clothes in a dryer.

The gowns arrived a few weeks before the wedding so my sister and I drove to Philly to pick them up. We didn't bother trying them on because we were having any necessary alterations done at home. When we finally tried them on, we were stunned. The halter-top part of the gown looked fantastic because we were well endowed but at least three inches of material was missing from the waist of the floor length skirt. The tailor sympathetically informed us that there wasn't enough time to order the material and alter the gowns in time for the wedding.

We called our niece and explained the dilemma. She loves us so much that she calmly recommended we try to find something sky blue that the two of us could wear. It was next to impossible finding one sky blue dress let alone two of them. Time was running out and we felt helpless. My young and slender colleague heard me whimpering about my situation and said, "Just go buy a pair of SPANX. I guarantee they'll take the inches off your waist and your gowns will fit fine." She told me that she wears SPANX every day for a smoother appearance. The 30 something mom couldn't weigh 100 pounds soaking wet. I had no other options so I left work early and headed to the mall. Trust me, finding a mall in NJ is never a problem.

There was only one store, at the time, which carried the Holy Grail of undergarments. I ran through the lingerie department searching for SPANX and finally found them resting along a corner wall. I grabbed my size and pessimistically entered the dressing room. I pulled the SPANX over my feet and cautiously inched them up my body. It was like stuffing ground meat into sausage casing. Beads of sweat formed on my forehead and armpits while words that a mother fears spewed from my unwitting mouth. I was determined to yank the *higher power* SPANX over my abdomen and up to my chest. I was persistent and eventually wrestled the giant condom over my fatty tissue until it reached the lower portion of my breastbone. I had met the enemy and he was mine! This undergarment promised to suppress the rear, thighs, and tummy; I needed it to suppress three inches off my waist.

I couldn't imagine going to the bathroom in this rubber suit, but I noticed a little *pee hole* in the cotton crotch and you know how much I love a cotton crotch. I drew a sigh of relief knowing that I wouldn't have to battle this latex warrior every time my alcohol consumption surpassed my bladder's liquid capacity.

My sister is built like me so I bought two pairs of SPANX since she was unable to make the trip. When I returned home, we tried on the gowns with our new body control undergarments. To our surprise, they fit like a glove. Not like Mike Tyson's boxing glove, more like Michael Jackson's white rhinestone glove. My friends it was nothing short of a miracle. SPANX had saved my niece's wedding.

My heart thanks you for reading my book. I happily shared my life with you and hopefully you saw a little of yourself in me. Remember to keep a song in your heart because a melody is a memory in the soundtrack of our lives.

        Your friend,

           Jane

IMAGE CREDITS

Images: GOOGLE and BING
License:
Free to share and use commercially

www.ingramcontent.com/pod-product-compliance
Lightning Source LLC
Chambersburg PA
CBHW061333040426
42444CB00011B/2892